Easton Lear to Save

A Children's Guide to Saving Money

Coloring and Activity Book

Written by: Rich Gomez
Illustrated by: Ashe Gomez
Contributions & inspired by: Easton Gomez

Felicity Fox Books Publishing House

Identifiers:

ISBN: 979-8-9860936-6-6

ISBN: 979-8-9860936-7-3

ISBN: 979-8-9860936-8-0

ISBN: 979-8-9860936-9-7

Available as a coloring book, paperback, hardback, and e-book

Easton Learns to Save

A Children's Guide to Saving Money

Coloring and Activity Book

Written by: Rich Gomez
Illustrated by: Ashe Gomez
Contributions & inspired by: Easton Gomez

Felicity Fox Books Publishing House

Easton loves to play with all his toys.

He has blocks, trucks, cars, and toys that show him things like counting and colors. Easton loves to learn and play with all of them every day.

When Easton goes to the store, he gets super excited looking at all the new toys.

There are so many to choose from!

YS

1,00
PIECE

BOOKS

A 1 S M
B 2 C A
C 3 I T

SLIME

Oh wow! What did Easton find?
He found a big red monster truck with
lights and sounds!

"Mom, dad! Can you buy this for me?"
Easton asked.
"How much is it?
Look at the sticker on it," she said.

Easton looked at the sticker.
"Six dollars!" he shouted.

"This is perfect for you to buy with your money," said dad.
"But I don't have money," Easton replied.

Then dad had a great idea!
"What if you learn to save money
and then come back and buy the truck?"

"I don't know what saving money is,
but I love learning new things,"
Easton told him.

The next day, dad tells Easton, "People save their money for different reasons. Sometimes it's for emergencies, and other times it's when they want to buy something big like a house or a vacation."

"Right now, you are saving to buy a toy, but we want to save so we can invest. Investing is having your money make money for you; I will teach you that next time."

"Money from a job that you do work for is called income. So, you will now have two types of chores, your regular daily chores that help mom and dad, and extra chores that you get paid for. The extra ones will be your job,

and doing that work is how you will receive your income. You will then put what we give you in your piggy bank right away to keep it safe, that is called paying yourself first, and that is how you save money."

Easton loves to help mom and dad with his regular chores, but this time he had extra work to start making income. So he started right away!

"Mom! What else can I help you with?" Easton asked. "After you pick up your toys, you can help me pick up everything off the floor so we can sweep and mop," mom said.

Easton was so excited to do extra work and be able to get an income!

Dad decided it was time to pay Easton and said, "Great job Easton! Here is some money for your work." Easton quickly ran and put it in his piggy bank, just like dad told him about paying himself first.

"Easton, I have some papers in the office that need to be picked up and thrown away," dad told him. It was a lot of work, but he got it all done. "Good job! The office looks nice and clean."

"Before you go, I have one more thing for you to do," dad mentioned. "Learning new things will help you make money later in life. So next, I want you to learn something new."

EASTONS
READING
CORNER

MATH

Easton loves learning new things, so he was so excited he could get money from it that he started learning right away.

4 + 2 = 6!

After he was done, dad gave him two dollars! "Wow! Two dollars!" Easton shouted. "When you learn new things, you can use it over and over to make more money. That's why learning makes more money than just doing a job once," dad said.

He ran to his piggy bank and placed both dollars inside.

CHA-CHING!

Easton kept doing extra work for mom and dad, but he always found new things to learn so he could make more.

Every time he got money, he would put it in his piggy bank right away. "I have to pay myself first!" he would say.

The following day mom said, "Easton, we are going to the store today; let's count your money." Mom and Easton love to count together. Mom opened Easton's piggy bank and took out all the money.

"That's a lot of dollars, mom!" Easton shouted with excitement."Yes, it is," mom said. "Let's count and see how much you have!"

Easton started counting his dollars.
"One, Two, Three, Four, Five, Six, Seven"

"Seven! I have seven dollars!" Easton shouted. "I have enough to buy the monster truck!" Easton was so excited because he had been working and saving up his money.

"I have seven dollars, dad!" Easton exclaimed. With a grin, dad said, "That's great! You have more than enough to buy the truck you wanted!" Easton couldn't wait to get to the store.

When he got there, Easton wanted to go get the truck first. "Dad, can we please go get my monster truck first?" Easton asked.

They all went to the toy section and got the truck first so that he could look at it while mom and dad shopped.

He was so excited he couldn't wait to get home, but he first had to pay for the monster truck.

Mom and dad were finally done,
and it was time to pay.

"When we get to the cashier, you give them your truck so they can scan it," dad explained. "Then they will tell you how much to give them."

The cashier scanned the truck and said," The total is $6.50." Easton gave her the seven dollars, and she gave him change. "I will teach you about taxes next time," dad told Easton.

He was so happy when he got home.
He played all day with his new toy.

"I love saving money!" Easton shouted with a big smile on his face.

ACTIVITIES!

Learn with Easton
with these activities!

Learn how to draw the piggy bank!

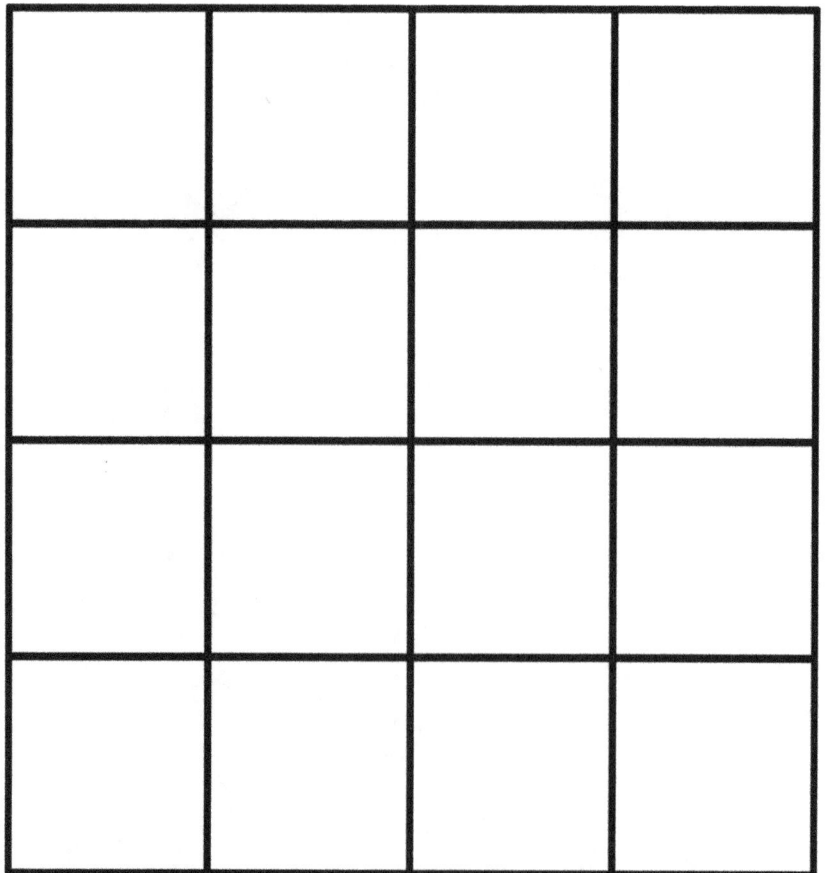

Count how much money is in the piggy bank!

$ _____

Match the price with the dollars!

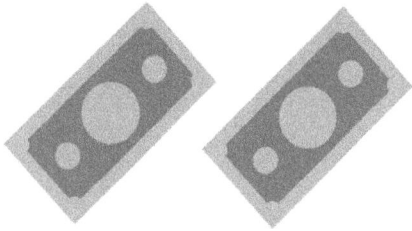

$4

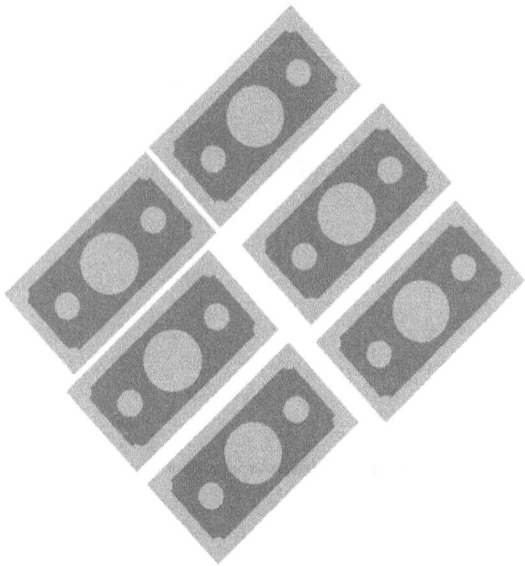

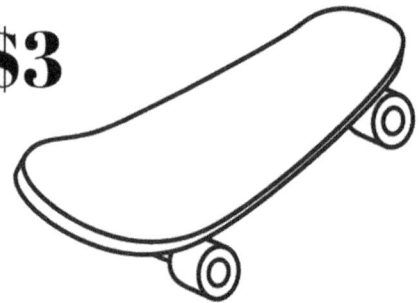

$3

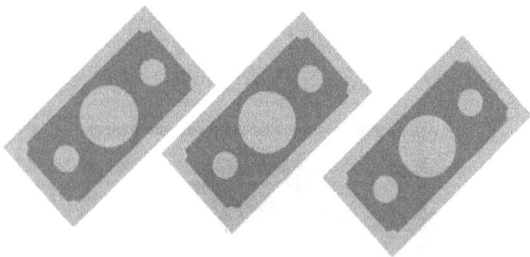

$6

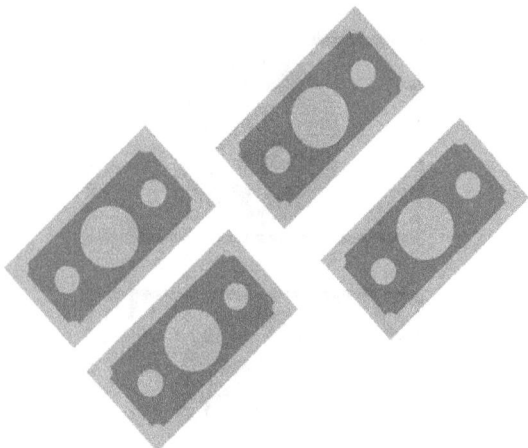

$2

Connect the dots to see the piggy bank!

5 6 7 8

1 2 4

3

28

27

9

26

25

10

24 21 20 11

16 15 12

17

23 22 19 18 14 13

Find the words below!

PIGGY BANK
CASHIER
LEARNING
STORE
SAVING

INVESTING
MONEY
WORK
TAXES
HELPING

COINS
TOYS
DOLLARS
PAY YOURSELF
INCOME

M	K	R	O	W	A	D	N	K	P	P	S	S	P
O	G	M	S	E	R	V	S	E	O	O	G	C	I
N	Y	L	Y	S	S	S	L	R	R	A	S	P	G
E	A	G	S	T	R	E	M	O	C	N	I	I	G
Y	T	G	P	A	R	A	O	T	S	W	L	S	Y
T	S	B	A	A	V	G	L	S	O	G	S	Y	B
L	S	N	I	O	C	I	M	L	N	A	N	O	A
G	Y	N	S	R	S	E	N	I	O	A	L	T	N
T	I	F	E	E	R	R	N	G	I	D	T	M	K
N	Y	A	X	W	O	R	E	G	I	S	O	C	F
G	Y	G	A	E	A	H	E	L	P	I	N	G	N
S	N	N	T	E	T	O	R	E	I	H	S	A	C
G	A	F	L	E	S	R	U	O	Y	Y	A	P	E
N	G	N	I	T	S	E	V	N	I	C	E	G	G

Help Easton find his way to his piggy bank!

Circle the toys that you have in your house!

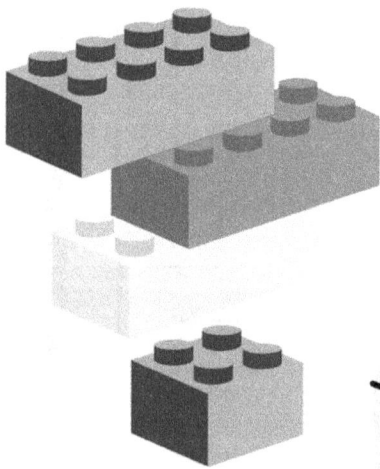

Find out what Easton will buy next!

Help Easton get to his toys!

Let's Learn About Coins!

COIN	FRONT	BACK	VALUE
Penny			**One Cent $ .01**
Nickel			**Five Cents $ .05**
Dime			**Ten Cents $ .10**
Quarter			**Twenty-Five Cents $ .25**
Four Quarters			**One Dollar $ 1.00**

Can you spot the differences?
There are 7 of them.

Cut out your own Easton bucks

THE UNITED STATES OF EASTON
IN GOD WE TRUST
ONE
ONE DOLLAR

THE UNITED STATES OF EASTON
IN GOD WE TRUST
ONE
ONE DOLLAR

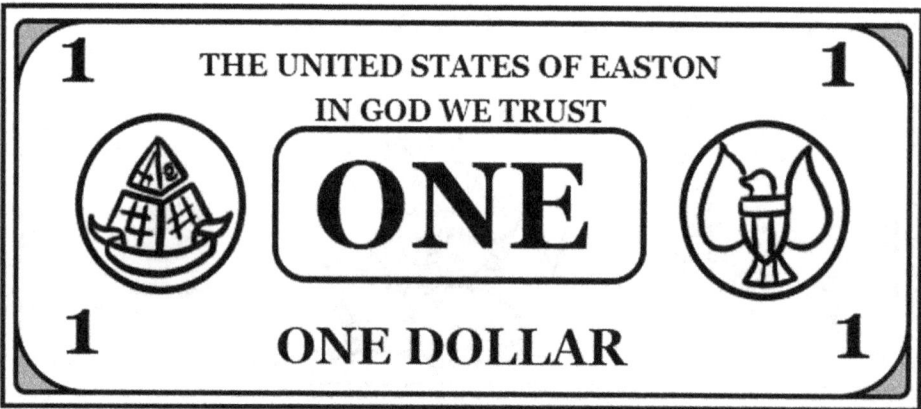

THE UNITED STATES OF EASTON
IN GOD WE TRUST
ONE
ONE DOLLAR

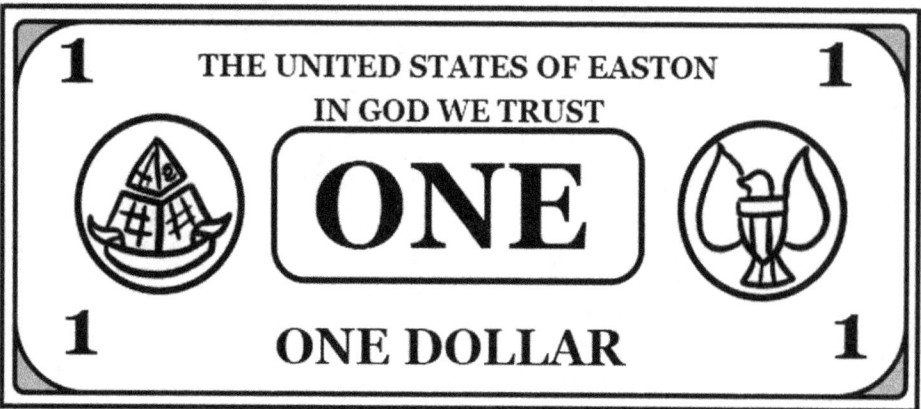

THE UNITED STATES OF EASTON
IN GOD WE TRUST
ONE
ONE DOLLAR

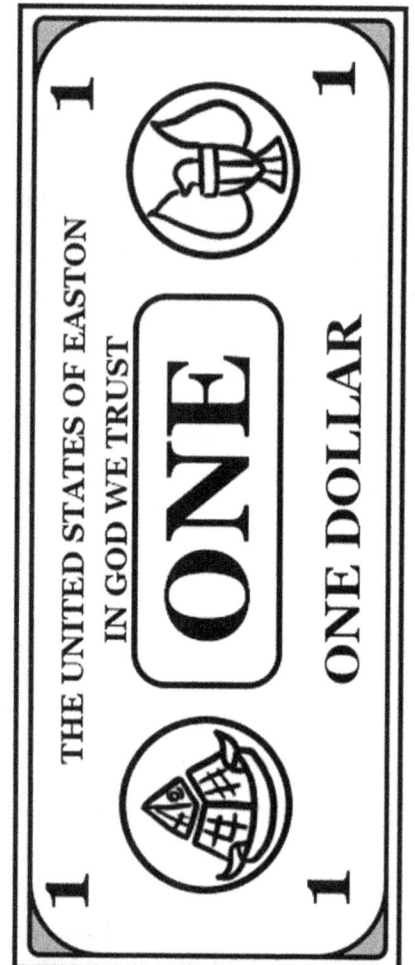

THE UNITED STATES OF EASTON
IN GOD WE TRUST
ONE
ONE DOLLAR

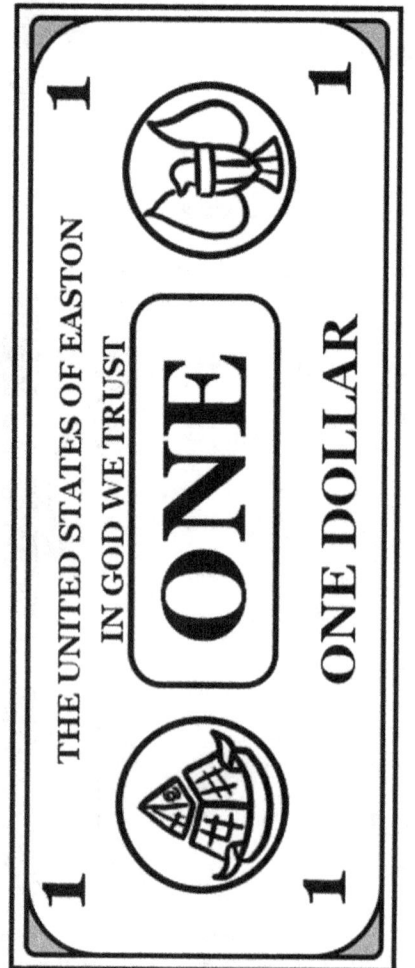

THE UNITED STATES OF EASTON
IN GOD WE TRUST
ONE
ONE DOLLAR

Easton can't wait to learn
about Budgeting Next!